W9-CAR-736

Mario Gomboli

The Fastest, Heaviest, Smallest, Largest, Fiercest, and Funniest

AMAZING ANIMALS

AN IMPRINT OF RUNNING PRESS
PHILADELPHIA • LONDON

First American edition published in the United States in 1994 by Courage Books

9 8 7 6 5 4 3 2
Digit on the right indicates the number of this printing

Library of Congress Cataloging-in-Publication Number 94-70953
ISBN 0-7624-0658-5

This book may be ordered by mail from the publisher
But try your bookstore first!

Published by Courage Books, an imprint of
Running Press Book Publishers
125 South Twenty-second Street
Philadelphia, Pennsylvania 19103-4399

Visit us on the web!
www.runningpress.com

CONTENTS

INTRODUCTION

Once upon a time there was a bird.
It was a funny little thing, about the same size as a goose but a bit fatter.
It had a beak almost like a parrot's, but a bit longer.
Its feet were like a chicken's, but a bit bigger, and although
it was a bird, it couldn't fly.
But the really sad thing about this bird is that it's extinct.
That means, there's none alive in the world at all.
The bird was called a dodo and it lived on just a few islands in the Indian Ocean.
When people went to live on those islands, they managed
to kill every single dodo.
No wonder they say "As dead as a dodo!"
Today people are much more thoughtful about animals, but some of them
are still in danger of becoming extinct.
The more you know about animals, the more you can do to help them
and stop them from ending up like the dodo.
Now enjoy the world of amazing animals that this book will open up to you.

DINOSAURS RULE!

Millions of years ago the earth was populated by some of the most amazing beasts ever—the dinosaurs. Today there are no dinosaurs alive, but people are still interested in what they were like. Do you know which was the largest, or the fiercest? The tallest, or the smallest? Here are some prehistoric records and other curious facts.

Brachiosaurus
Quetzalcoatlus
Diplodocus
Pachycephalosaurus
Ankylosaurus
Stegosaurus
cosaurus

THE MOST TALKED ABOUT

STEGOSAURUS (30 feet long from nose to tail; weighed 4 tons. Lived about 160 million years ago). The stegosaurus may look quite fierce in pictures but, in fact, it didn't eat meat. The only weapon it had to protect itself from other dinosaurs was its tail which had bony spikes at the end of it. Scientists are always talking about the stegosaurus because they don't really know much about it. Nobody knows what the plates on its back were for. They think that they might have been for controlling body temperature, so that the dinosaur didn't get too hot or too cold. They aren't even sure what the stegosaurus really looked like. However, they do know that it was quite stupid because, even though it was so big, its brain was as small as a dog's!

THE TALLEST

BRACHIOSAURUS (40 feet high; 50 tons. Lived about 160 million years ago). The brachiosaurus was about as high as a four-story building and as heavy as a train, yet this was also a peaceful dinosaur. They lived in groups by lakes and ponds, feeding on grasses and other plants.

THE SMALLEST

COMPSOGNATHUS ($1\frac{1}{2}$ feet long; 7 pounds. Lived about 160 million years ago). The compsognathus is the smallest dinosaur ever found, being only about the size of a chicken. It was a very fast runner and used its speed to hide from larger and stronger hunters.

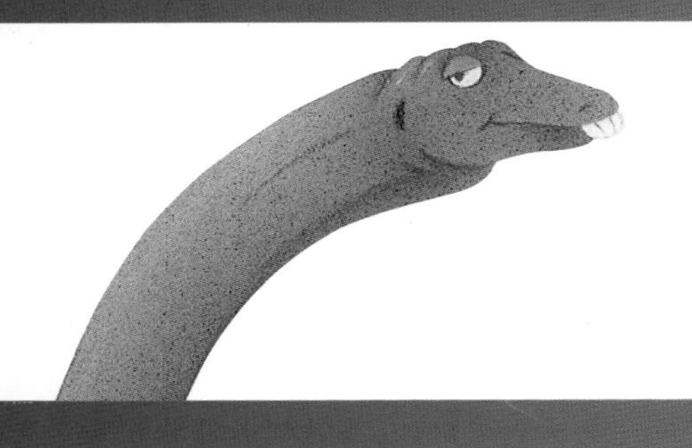

THE LONGEST

DIPLODOCUS (90 feet long; 10 tons. Lived about 160 million years ago). From the tip of its nose to the end of its tail the diplodocus was about as long as seven cars parked in a line. Some scientists think it needed a second brain to help control its huge body. It lived on land and was a plant eater.

THE MOST ARMOR-PLATED

ANKYLOSAURUS (11 feet long; 1,500 pounds. Lived about 100 million years ago). The ankylosaurus might have been smaller than a lot of other dinosaurs, but it was one of the best protected. It was like a miniature army tank, covered in thick, bony plates and spikes. This plant eater could also keep off attackers by lashing out with the hard ball on the end of its tail.

THE MOST "OBSTINATE"

PACHYCEPHALOSAURUS (15 feet long; 900 pounds. Lived about 100 million years ago). The pachycephalosaurus had the thickest skull of all the dinosaurs. In fact, his name means ´thick-headed reptile´! These dinosaurs used to fight by head-butting each other, so they needed good protection for their brains.

THE GREATEST FLIER

QUETZALCOATLUS (40 feet across the wings; 140 pounds. Lived about 100 million years ago). The quetzalcoatlus was about the size of a small aircraft. It was forced to stay in the air most of the time, for its long claws made taking off difficult. It rested hanging upside down in a cave, like modern bats.

THE FIERCEST

TYRANNOSAURUS REX (46 feet long; 9 tons. Lived about 100 million years ago). The tyrannosaurus has been called "the most terrible killing machine that ever tramped the earth." It was a fierce hunter and few dinosaurs were safe when it was hungry. Its back legs were very strong, making it a fast runner, and its mouth was full of sharp teeth as long as knives. No one really knows what its little front legs were for–they may have helped it to get up off the ground after sleeping.

THE MOST DELICATE

PSITTACOSAURUS (3 inches; 7 ounces. Lived about 100 million years ago). The only remains of the psittacosaurus that have been found are of a baby, but scientists think that this dinosaur was about as big as a turkey when fully grown. Its skull had a horny beak on the tip of the nose and its name means 'parrot reptile'. It was a plant eater that used the beak to cut off its food which it then held in its front legs to eat.

THE FUNNIEST

PARASAUROLOPHUS (30 feet long; 3 tons. Lived about 100 million years ago). The parasaurolophus lived in packs and was a very strange-looking dinosaur, with a long, hollow crest on the top of its head. The crest contained breathing tubes which probably helped the parasaurolophus to smell and taste its food before eating. Scientists also think the crest was used to make honking sounds to other members of the pack.

THE MOST FAMOUS

TRICERATOPS (30 feet long; 8 tons. Lived about 100 million years ago). The triceratops is surely the most famous prehistoric reptile and more is known about it than any other dinosaur. Its fierce appearance, with its three horns, sturdy armored collar and aggressive look, makes it seem like a real monster. But really this beast was a peaceful plant eater and its armor was used to defend itself from meat-eating dinosaurs.

NOAH'S ARK

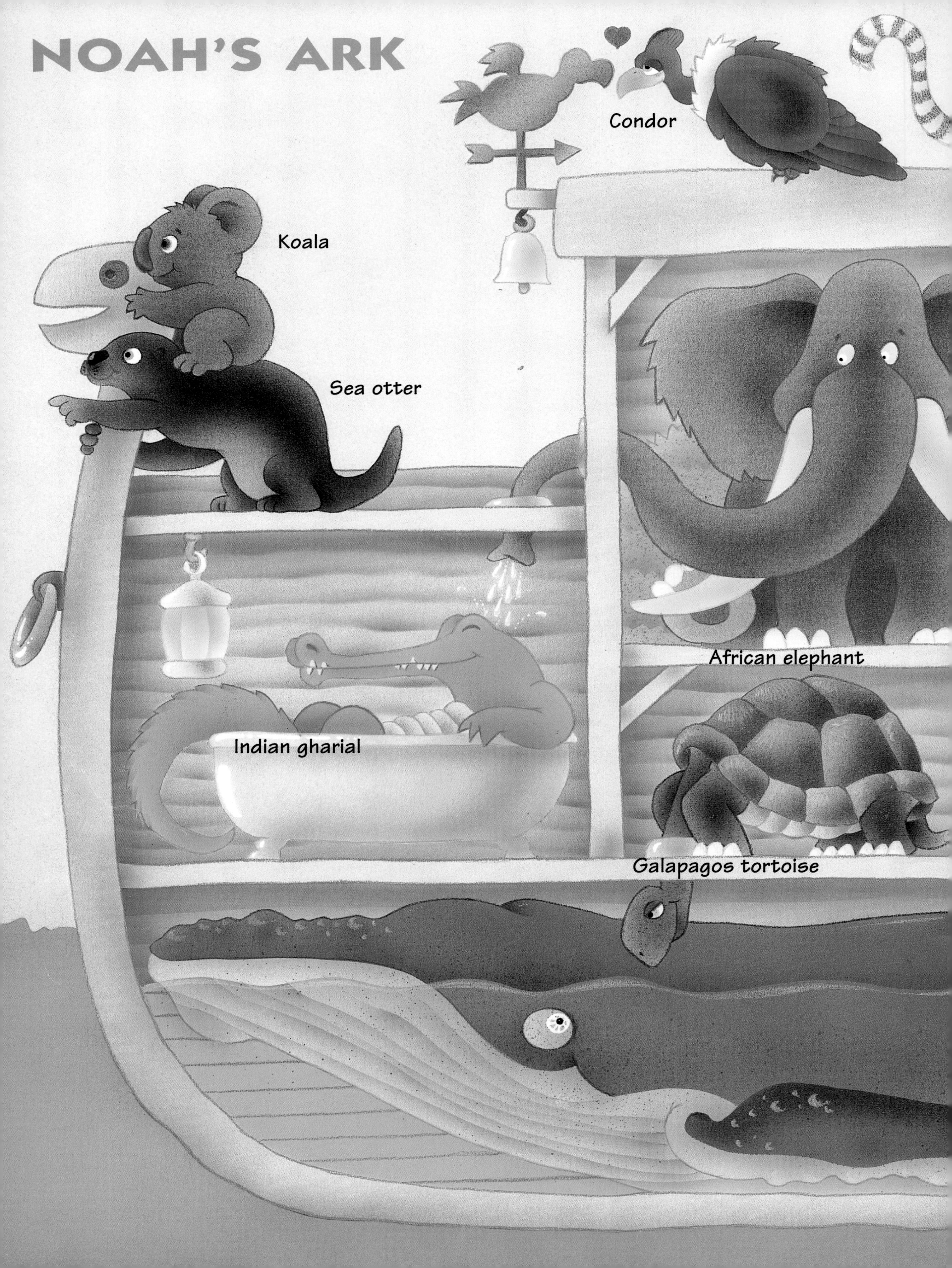

Condor
Koala
Sea otter
African elephant
Indian gharial
Galapagos tortoise

No one really knows what killed the dinosaurs. Today the world is full of animals which are also in danger of dying out. This is because they are being hunted, or because their homes are being destroyed.

If Noah were to build a new Ark today, these are some of the animals he might choose to rescue.

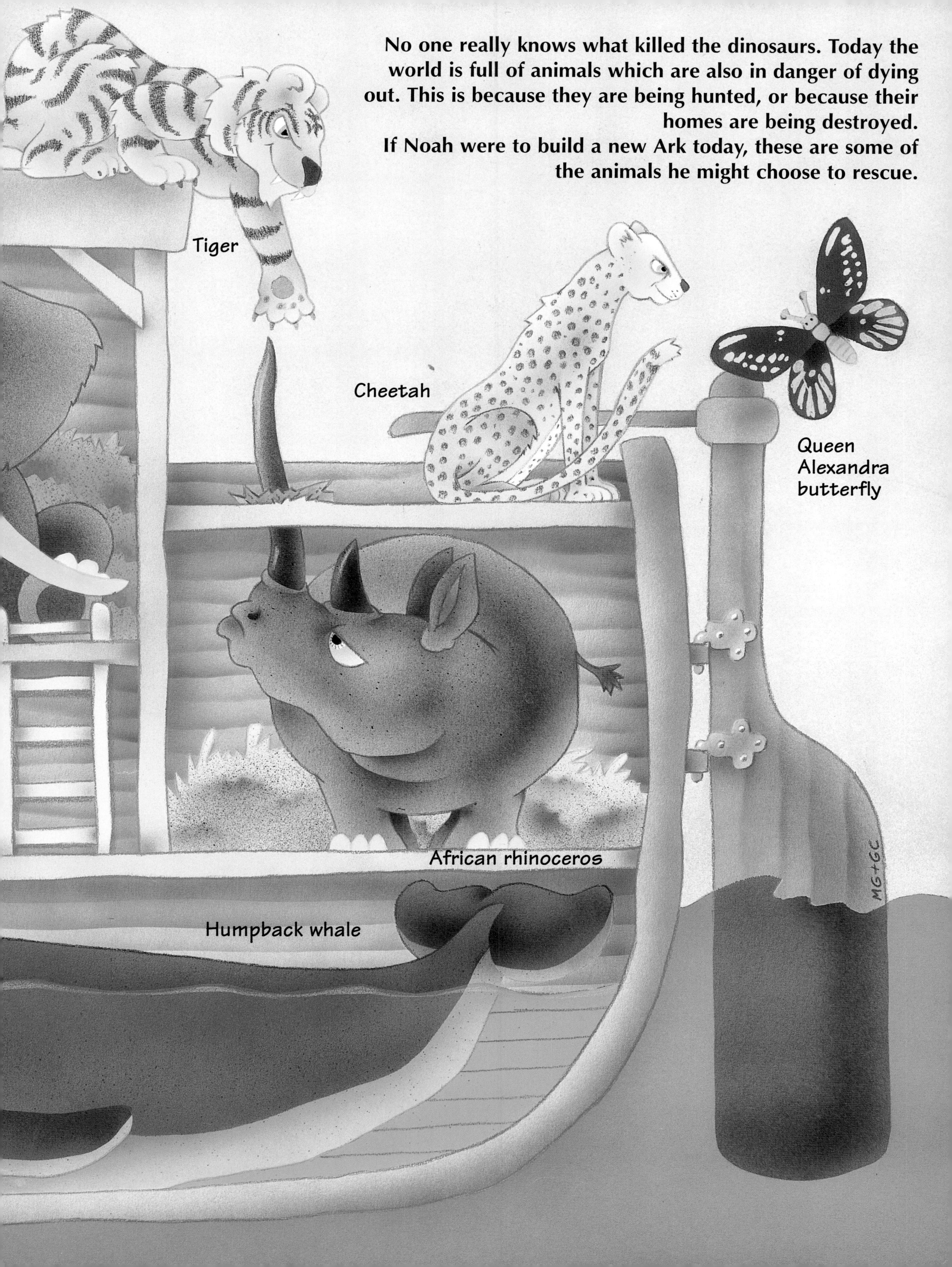

THE LARGEST

The AFRICAN ELEPHANT is the largest four-legged land animal in the world. A male elephant can be as tall as 12 feet and weigh as much as 6 tons. Many elephants now live in protected parks, but hunters still creep in to kill them. They cut off their tusks, which are made of ivory, and sell them secretly. The ivory is used to make expensive jewelry and ornaments.

THE UGLIEST

The CONDOR lives mainly in South America. This is an enormous bird with wings which measure over 10 feet from tip to tip. Today there are only about a hundred condors left in the world because they have been hunted by people who want to collect their eggs and feathers. They only lay one egg every two years.

THE HARDEST

The GALAPAGOS TORTOISE can measure up to 5 feet long and weigh up to 300 pounds. Sailors used to catch these gentle giants for food, but they ate so many they nearly disappeared. Now hunting them is not allowed.

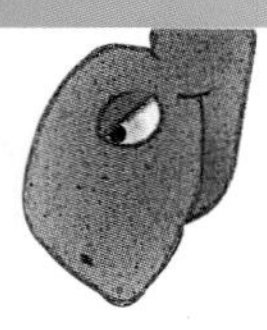

THE FASTEST

The CHEETAH can run faster than any other animal, around 60 miles per hour over short distances. Unfortunately they are not fast enough to escape from the hunters, who trap them for zoos or kill them for their beautiful skins. Most live in protected areas of Central Africa but they are still in great danger.

THE MOST CROWDED-OUT

The GHARIAL is being squeezed out of its home. These crocodiles once lived happily in the rivers of India. Now so many people live on the banks, there's hardly any room left for the gharial.

THE MOST LIKABLE

Everyone loves the furry KOALA who lives in Australia. They are well looked after and protected, but they are still in danger from bush fires and because the eucalyptus trees which provide their food are becoming rare.

THE SOFTEST

The SEA OTTER spends its life mostly in the water, often having its babies on rafts of seaweed instead of on land. It is in danger because of its lovely fur coat. Hunters have driven the otters far away from their natural homes, and many die from oil spills from commercial tankers.

THE MOST INNOCENT

There are two types of AFRICAN RHINOCEROS, the black rhino and the white rhino. This creature is in danger for the stupidest reason. Nobody wants to eat it, or to use its skin; they simply want to take the horn from the end of its nose because they believe it brings good luck and good health. People will pay hunters a lot of money for that 'magic' horn.

THE MOST BEAUTIFUL

The QUEEN ALEXANDRA BUTTERFLY lives in New Guinea. These colorful insects have wings larger than a dinner plate. They are in danger because their forest homes are being destroyed, and also because collectors are eager to catch these lovely butterflies and display them in glass cases.

THE FIERCEST

The TIGER is the fiercest and largest big cat; it is about 9 feet in length, 3 feet of which is its tail! They are splendid swimmers and have excellent hearing, which helps them to stalk their food. The tiger is in most danger from the fiercest hunter of all—man! There are now so few tigers left that a special plan has been set up to try and save them.

THE HEAVIEST

The HUMPBACK WHALE weighs tons and tons—in fact, it's as big as a railroad engine! In spite of its size, this whale eats only tiny shrimp-like creatures called krill. Even though they are now protected by law, humpback whales are still hunted in some parts of the world. Oil leaks are probably also helping to kill these giants of the seas.

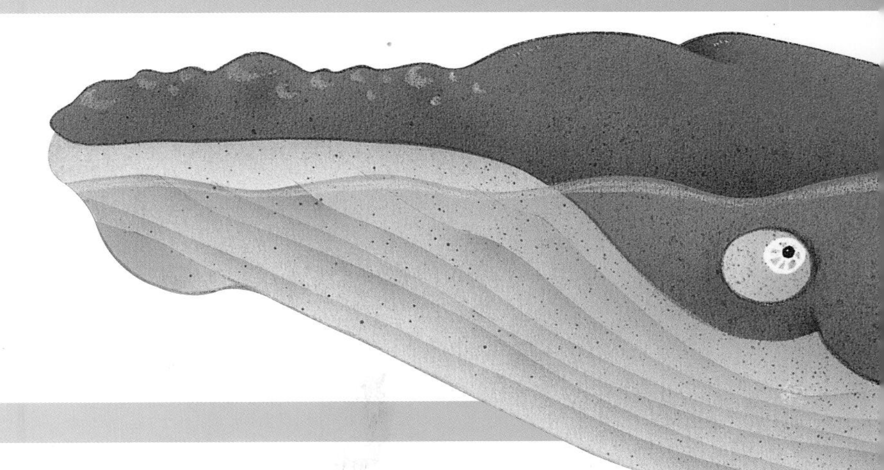

Skua
Killer whale
Emperor penguin
Leopard seal
Krill
Starfish

CHAMPIONS OF THE ANTARCTIC

The South Pole is one of the coldest places in the world. Yet between its icebergs swim all sorts of creatures, large and small, all able to live quite happily in this freezing place.

THE WORST REPUTATION

The KILLER WHALE is a frightening sight and a fierce hunter. Male killer whales can be up to 33 feet long and are so strong that they are able to leap right out of the water. The long fin on its back is about 3 feet long and is so sharp that it can pierce a shark´s skin. It is a deadly hunter, it even attacks whales larger than itself. But the killer whale is also very intelligent and can actually be quite peaceful, friendly and even playful, like his dolphin relations.

THE GREEDIEST

The SKUA is a bird a little larger than a dove, about one and a half feet long and weighing 2 pounds. It flies better than a seagull and is as hungry as an eagle who has not eaten for six months! The skua eats everything from prawns to penguin eggs, from baby chicks to animal corpses. It is not strong enough to attack large creatures so sometimes it robs food from the mouths of others and can be a real bully. It sweeps away anything it finds that might be edible, so it's also quite good at keeping its home clean!

THE COLDEST

The ICE FISH is able to defend itself from the most terrible enemy: the intense polar cold. Its blood is ice-white in color and contains a special substance to stop the fish from becoming a solid block of ice—a bit like anti-freeze for cars! The ice fish needs a strong, large heart, double the size of any similar fish, to pump the blood around its body.

THE FIERCEST

The LEOPARD SEAL with its spotty fur coat looks like a lovable, cuddly animal, but it is a deadly hunter. With a body that is longer than 10 feet and weighing about half a ton, it is almost the size of a small car. This seal's most deadly weapon is its mouth: it is so big that it can swallow a small penguin whole, in one gulp! It also has a fine set of sharp teeth. The leopard seal sometimes jumps out of the water onto an ice slab where penguins are gathered, using its weight to tilt the island and slide its lunch straight into its mouth.

THE TINIEST

The KRILL is a little prawn that you can almost see through. It is only a fraction of an inch long, yet it is the favorite food of many animals in the Antarctic. These tiny creatures live in enormous groups, and there are far too many of them to count. A whale can eat thousands of krill in one mouthful, yet there are always plenty more to go round. Scientists are even trying to find ways of using krill to help feed the starving people of the world.

THE UGLIEST

The ELEPHANT SEAL weighs more than 3 tons and is over 20 feet long. It looks like a pyramid of solid fat. It gets its name from its large trunk-like nose, which is as long as an arm. The elephant seal has a loud and ugly voice and moves very clumsily on land. However, in the water, it swims as speedily and gracefully as any other seal. The male seal is always arguing with the other males, and he uses his pointed teeth as deadly weapons. However, he prefers not to kill his rivals and likes to show off noisily when he has won a fight. Female elephant seals are much smaller and friendlier. One male might have as many as 80 wives in his group!

THE FRIENDLIEST

STARFISH like these live in families of hundreds that stand out like brilliant long red ribbons on the black sandy floor of the Atlantic Ocean. They look as if they are walking in a row, but really they travel very little. They gently move with the water, catching the little scraps of food that are carried along in the flow.

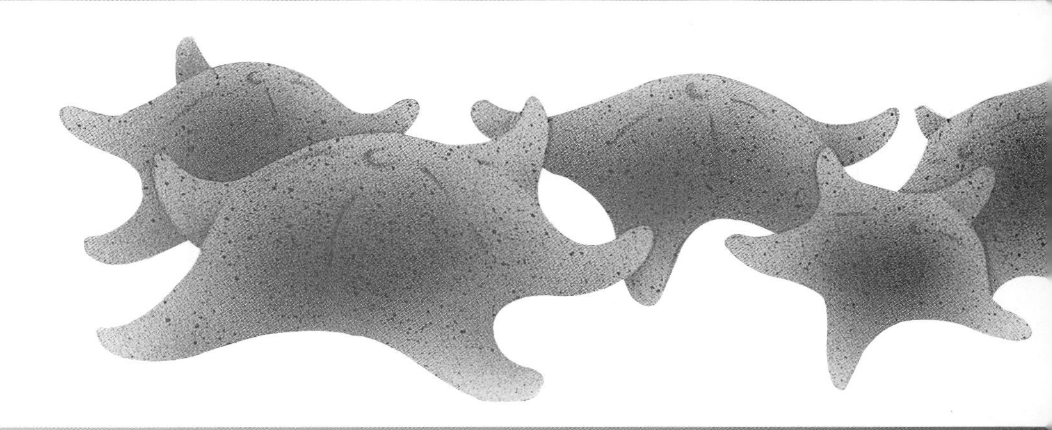

THE MOST ELEGANT

The EMPEROR PENGUIN travels around on the icebergs of the Antarctic looking as if it were at a very smart party. It is definitely the best-dressed penguin, in its sleek 'dinner jacket' and orange 'neck tie'. It is also the tallest penguin (measuring almost 5 feet) and the slimmest (weighing less than 65 pounds). And they don't need babysitters—they take their eggs with them, keeping them warm between their legs.

Late at night, when the moon is in the sky, all sorts of strange creatures creep out from their homes. They are not vampires or werewolves, but real animals that we could all meet if we missed a little sleep. Our night is their day, and they all live very busy lives.

Bat

Nightjar

Owl

Firefly

MG+LB

Long-eared owl

Barn owl

Emperor moth

Little owl

Badger

Hedgehog

THE MOST ELEGANT

The BADGER has the most beautiful black and white fur coat, and almost looks as if it's wearing a mask. Although it is only about 3 feet long, it has short, powerful legs and strong claws on its front paws. It is a very good digger and lives underground in a home called a "set." Badgers mostly eat earthworms, but they also like grass and nuts, and creatures such as insects, snails and mice.

THE BRIGHTEST

While most animals who come out at night do their best to keep themselves hidden, the FIREFLY shines brightly at night. This little beetle gives off a yellow glow from its rear end, although these lights are only flashed for moments at a time. This is probably the fireflies' way of talking to each other. In some places they are called 'lightning bugs'. The light they give off is so strong that sometimes people capture these insects and use them to make lanterns.

THE QUIETEST

The BARN OWL has very soft feathers at the ends of its wings, which make it able to fly very quietly. People have often been frightened by the barn owl, with its ghostly white face, swooping silently overhead. It is a deadly hunter with very good eyesight, which means it can spot and pounce on a mouse or rat before its victim has even noticed. Even if the moon is not out, its sharp ears can hear the faintest rustle in the dark.

THE BEST EQUIPPED

The BAT is the only mammal that can fly, although it can't walk very well. When it is not in flight, it hangs upside down from the roofs of caves or branches of trees. Bats do have good eyesight and a good sense of smell, but they also have a special kind of 'radar' system that helps them to catch insects and fly in the dark without bumping into anything.

THE MOST TIMID

The HEDGEHOG is a shy little animal who likes to stay out of trouble. It will eat almost anything, but it likes slugs, snails, insects and worms best. If an enemy comes near, the hedgehog will roll up into a tight, prickly ball that no other creature can disturb.

THE GREEDIEST

The NIGHTJAR is as big as a swallow but much hungrier. Its mouth is always open, ready to swallow all the insects that fly by. Its good eyesight helps it to avoid swallowing the wrong things and it has a beak surrounded by sensitive hairs, capable of telling the difference between a tasty mosquito and a poplar seed.

THE LAZIEST

The LITTLE OWL (or dwarf owl) is not much bigger than the span of a hand. Many little owls live in the Northwest United States, but they are so lazy that they cannot be bothered to build proper nests. Instead they make their homes in bushes or holes that other animals have abandoned. They don't even line them with feathers to make them cosy for the babies!

THE MOST PRAISED

The LONG-EARED OWL is often thought of as a wise old bird. Perhaps this is because it looks as though it wears spectacles, for this was once thought to be a sign of intelligence. Perhaps it is because it often looks as if it were thinking—when in fact it has probably spotted a tasty meal and is just waiting for the right time to pounce. Perhaps it is because it chooses to eat food that farmers think are pests—snakes, rats and so on. Whatever the reason, you can be sure its long ears pick up every sound around.

THE MOST BEAUTIFUL

The EMPEROR MOTH is one of the largest moths in Italy, with large wings that measure about 6 inches, the size of a small plate. At sunset the fluttering males meet up and look for females, which are always hiding in the bushes! The adults never eat, and die as soon as they have laid their eggs. Farmers do not like these moths, for the larvae which hatch from their eggs damage fruit trees. Because of this, the Emperor moth has become quite rare.

THE MOST INSULTED

Throughout history, OWLS have been thought of as unlucky birds. Because they fly at night and make eerie, hooting calls, they seem very mysterious and people sometimes said that they were witches in disguise. When owls eat the small mammals they catch, they swallow them whole. Later they spit out the bits they don't want—the bones, teeth and skin—all neatly wrapped up in a parcel. These are called owl pellets and they can often be found on the ground underneath an owl's nest.

FUNNY FACES

Shoebill
Crocodile
Tasmanian
Egg-eating snake
Duck-billed platpus
Shark
MG+EC

Have you ever looked into the mirror and pulled a funny face? In the animal kingdom you will of the oddest faces you will ever see, and all made by nature.

THE BIGGEST MOUTH

(So big that we couldn't fit it on this page) belongs to the BLUE WHALE. But even though it has such a big mouth, it doesn't have sharp teeth; instead it has a 'gate' made of whalebone called 'baleen'. This animal is a real giant, measuring up to 100 feet in length and weighing 135 tons—that's as heavy as twenty elephants! In spite of its size, it eats only krill and plankton—masses of tiny creatures smaller than ants. It fills its mouth with water, lowers the gate and then lets out the liquid, swallowing the food. Clever, isn't it?

THE LONGEST MOUTH

The mouth of a CROCODILE can easily be longer than a human arm. It will happily snap its jaws on any fish or small animals that happen to pass within reach, but if it catches a larger creature it often drags it back to its lair where it will rot, making it easier to eat. Sometimes male crocodiles will open their mouths wide and make a sound a bit like a drum-roll. This is to attract any female crocodiles that might be near.

THE MOST USEFUL MOUTH

The PELICAN probably has the most useful mouth of any bird. On first glance its mouth might seem like any old beak—long and hooked—but the lower part of the bill is made of stretchy skin. The pelican uses this as a fishing bucket. It dives under the surface of the sea and scoops up as much as it can. Then it rests somewhere, pours out the water and eats the fish. This is particularly handy for mother pelicans, who use it to carry plenty of fresh, wriggling fish to their young.

THE HUNGRIEST MOUTH

The TASMANIAN DEVIL lives only on the island of Tasmania, near Australia, and its jaws are always on the go! Similar to a fat and sturdy mouse, but the size of a dog, this animal is quite ugly. It is a very fierce hunter. During the day it sleeps in its den, well hidden between the rocks, but at night it hunts birds and reptiles. It usually hunts alone, but can also be seen feeding in packs from the dead bodies of large animals.

THE MOUTH WITH THE MOST TEETH

The FROG FISH is a long thin fish, 6 feet long, that lives in the depths of the Mediterranean Sea and Atlantic Ocean. It has hundreds of teeth, even on the roof of its mouth, throat and tongue. Most of the time these teeth lie flat, but when the frog fish attacks, they spring up and sink firmly into its prey. It has two long feelers on top of its head which help it to sense when other fish are near.

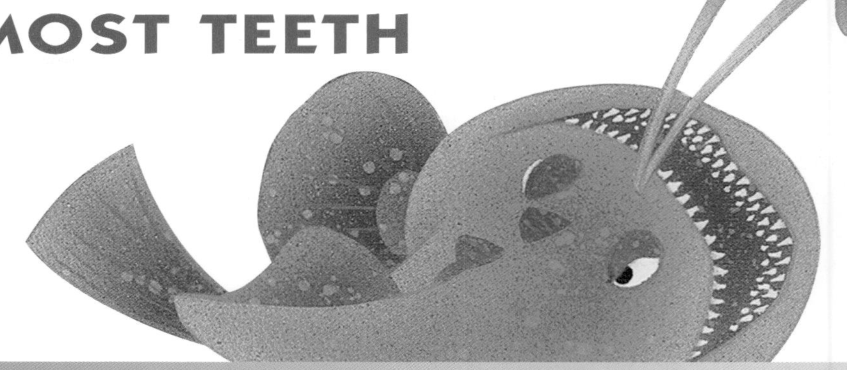

THE UGLIEST MOUTH

The SHOEBILL's mouth looks exactly like a Dutch wooden clog. This bird uses its shaped beak to make its nest of mud and dry twigs. It is also used as a shovel to dig for food in the marsh land where it lives. The shoebill doesn't have a voice, but sometimes it bangs the two parts of its beak together, making a noise just like that of two wooden clogs being knocked against each other.

THE GREEDIEST MOUTH

The EGG-EATING SNAKE has a head much smaller than the eggs that it tries to eat. So how does it do it? This snake has a special jaw which stretches like elastic and, thanks to this, it manages to swallow eggs three times larger than its body. Then it crushes the egg and spits out the shell. But the egg-eating snake doesn't eat just any old eggs—first it uses its tongue to test whether the eggs are fresh!

THE MOST TREACHEROUS MOUTH

This belongs to the MORAY EEL. This extraordinary fish is armed with dozens of very sharp teeth that point backwards, like hooks. So, whatever it bites can never escape. Moray eels are very fast and strong, and some of them can even poison their victims.

THE ODDEST MOUTH

The DUCK-BILLED PLATYPUS looks like a beaver with a duck's bill stuck on the front. The platypus is an all-round oddity, for it produces milk for its young like a mammal, yet lays eggs like a bird and has webbed feet! Unlike a duck, however, the bill is covered with a sensitive skin which helps it to hunt for worms, shellfish, and insects.

THE MOST FRIGHTENING MOUTH

When the SHARK's mouth is wide open, it practically turns the shark into a tunnel, able to swallow any prey that gets in its way. Sharks have rows and rows of triangular teeth, all sharper than steak knives. Sharks need to move in order to breathe, so they need to eat continually and their mouths are constantly active. However, not all sharks are dangerous. For example, the basking shark is totally harmless, in spite of its enormous size; the whale shark is as long as a fishing boat and as heavy as a lorry, but has almost no teeth and eats only plankton, jellyfish, and prawns.

WE ARE THE CHAMPIONS!

If you could pick your ideal soccer team made up of players from the animal kingdom, who would you choose to play? We think that this line-up would prove to be World Cup Champions.

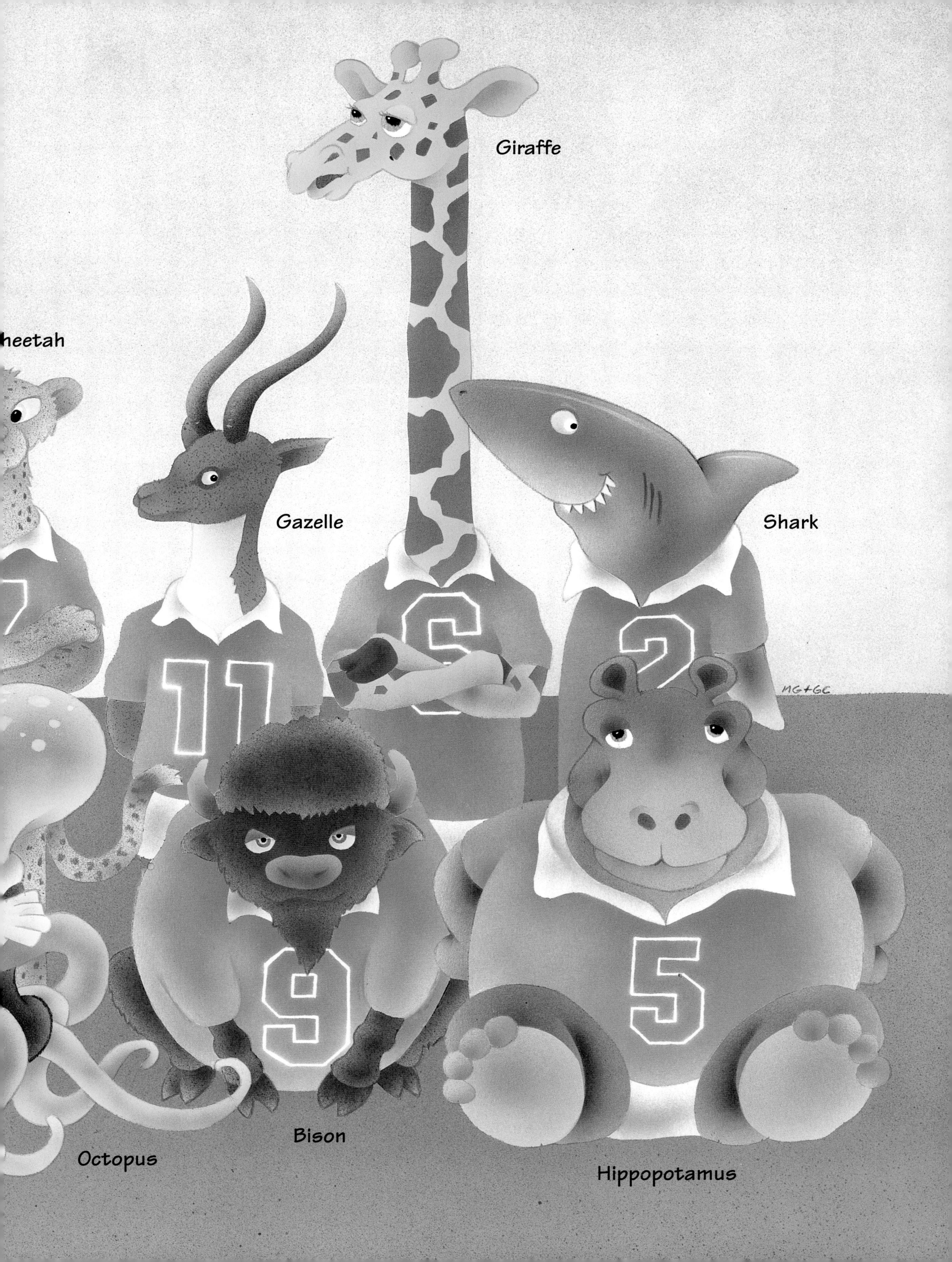
Giraffe
heetah
Gazelle
Shark
11
2
9
5
Bison
Octopus
Hippopotamus

The EAGLE is a powerful bird with strong wings, long claws (or talons) and perfect eyesight. It loves to fly high above the world, always on the lookout and ready to pounce. It has a quick-thinking brain and never misses a trick. The eagle is rarely aggressive—a hard blow from its beak or claws soon sorts out lunch, but often a screeching cry from this bird is enough to freeze the blood in the veins of anything nearby, enemy or friend. These characteristics make the eagle an ideal trainer for the team.

The BISON is not famous for its intelligence, but for its stubbornness and ability to run, sweeping away any obstacles or enemies in its path. It likes to be in a group and blindly follows the directions of the head of the herd. Its enormous body supports him even during long gallops and makes him devastating to his attackers. The bison would make an unbeatable center-forward.

The GORILLA possesses incredible strength, is very intelligent and can be aggressive or peaceful to get what it wants. With its broad chest, muscular neck and strong hands and feet, the gorilla would be a perfect left back.

The BROWN BEAR picks out its territory and defends it to the last. It senses an intruder immediately and fends it off. Few creatures can stand up to its size, intelligence, and determination, making the brown bear a fearsome right mid-field player.

The CHEETAH is all nerve and muscle, always tense and ready to spring. In open ground it moves swiftly and speedily, as silent as it is fast, suddenly appearing where it is least expected. At that point its deadly attack allows nothing to escape. Its sharp eyesight is able to spot the slightest error and its intelligence allows it to out-think most of its opponents. The cheetah would make a deadly player, a very dangerous right wing.

The OSTRICH may be a bird, but it can't fly; however, it can run very well. About 6 feet in height, it dominates and controls its territory. It has strong lungs and powerful muscles that enable it to keep up under pressure, never losing speed. If running is not enough, the ostrich can also kick violently. If it is still in difficulty, it plumps up its strong feathers to make itself look even bigger and tougher. The ostrich might look like an odd player, but he would make an exceptional right half-back.

The FOX is cunning and nothing escapes his bright eyes. He is quick, clever, and often surprising. The team can't do without him as a half-back.

The GAZELLE runs and jumps to meet any challenge. It certainly knows how to spring and reacts to the actions of anything running nearby. Its slender, but fit body enables it to take advantage of any mistakes its opponents might make. The gazelle would make a fine left wing.

The SHARK is always fast and aggressive, strong and resistant, and can keep going without a break for hours. It also has patience, meaning it never gives up on any opponents. At the first sign of difficulty, the shark is ready to move in for the kill. Very competitive and persistent, the shark would make a perfect right full-back.

The GIRAFFE, naturally, looks down on everyone from above. Its excellent hearing means it is always alert for any sign of danger, but its true strength is in its long legs which are good at running and kicking. When necessary it can also score with a perfect header. The giraffe is not aggressive, but it will not permit intruders into its territory unchallenged, making it a valuable striker.

The HIPPOPOTAMUS uses its mass of muscles and fat as a deadly weapon, capable of stopping or repelling any attack. Often just its presence is enough to discourage its opponents, forcing them to think of ways to get around it, rather than challenging it directly. The hippopotamus might look bulky and slow, but when needed it can be an unexpectedly good runner, agile and fast. An unpassable center full-back.

Armed with eight long tentacles, each with hundreds of suckers, the OCTOPUS is capable of grabbing anything that moves! It is also one of the most intelligent and creative of creatures, always thinking well ahead of its enemies. It prefers to stay in one place, but if necessary it does not hesitate to leave its territory to avoid danger, returning to its den as soon as possible. The octopus is able to stay perfectly still for a long time, then pounces with the speed of a snake at the right moment. No prizes for guessing what position the octopus holds—it's an absolutely unbeatable goalie!

LOOKING AFTER BABY

Animals look after their babies in all sorts of ways. All of these animals are very unusual parents. Can you see how they care for their babies?

Italian tarantula
Kangaroo
Beaver

THE MOST WELL KNOWN

The most patient mother is the KANGAROO. She keeps her baby in a pouch on the front of her stomach. When the baby roo (or joey) is born, it is as small as a beetle! It lives in her pouch, feeding and growing, for the first six months of its life. Even when it is big enough to come out to play, it always stays close to its mother, ready to jump back into her pouch if it gets frightened, tired or hungry.

THE MOST PATIENT

The most patient mother is a large spider called the ITALIAN TARANTULA. She lays hundreds of eggs, but she never leaves them alone in her nest. Instead, she carries them with her all the time until the babies are born.

THE MOST CAREFUL MOTHER

The most careful mother is the TILAPIA FISH. She has to be careful because she hides her eggs in her mouth. Even when they are born, the baby fish still swim in and out of mom's or dad's mouth. People used to think that they were eating their babies, but they are really protecting them.

THE FUNNIEST

The funniest group must be the SHREW family. Shrew babies are born blind and without fur, so they don't leave the nest right away. As soon as her babies can see and walk, the mother teaches them to hold onto each other with their teeth. Then they go out, all joined together in a long train with mom at the front.

THE MOST RESTLESS

The most restless mother is a bird called the WOODCOCK. Mother woodcock sits still on her nest for a whole month, making sure that her eggs are safe. Her brown feathers help her to hide from enemies that might be looking out for a tasty meal. But when the babies are hatched, she is always on the move, looking for the best place to keep her family. If there is danger, mom carries each chick to safety in her beak or claws.

THE MOST PROTECTIVE

The most protective mother is the VERVET MONKEY. She is tiny, but if a lion comes too close to her baby she frightens him away by screaming loudly, and jumping and baring her teeth. Her baby holds on tightly with its tiny hands, gripping the fur on her stomach as she leaps from branch to branch in the trees. If the baby dares to let go, she gets cross and smacks it!

THE STRANGEST BABY SITTER

The strangest baby sitter is the MIDWIFE TOAD. In this family, dad looks after the eggs. He wraps them around his back legs like a string of beads and carries them around like a knapsack. For three weeks he carries the eggs, resting in his burrow during the day and feeding at night. He keeps the eggs damp and cool until it is time for the tadpoles to hatch out and start swimming.

THE MOTHER WHO HAS TO DO THE MOST TEACHING

The mother who has to do the most teaching is the BEAVER. Baby beavers are also born blind and without fur. When they are old enough they learn to walk, and then they have to learn how to swim. Mother beaver teaches them to swim, holding them up in the water until they are able to paddle about on their own. Later they will even have to learn how to cut down trees and build their own houses!

PRIME PRIMATES

Primates are mammals that have good brains, can stand on two feet for a long time, have skillful hands and eyes set side by side at the front of their heads. Human beings are primates—and so are monkeys and apes. Like humans, there are all sorts of different monkeys and apes, and here you will meet just a few of them.

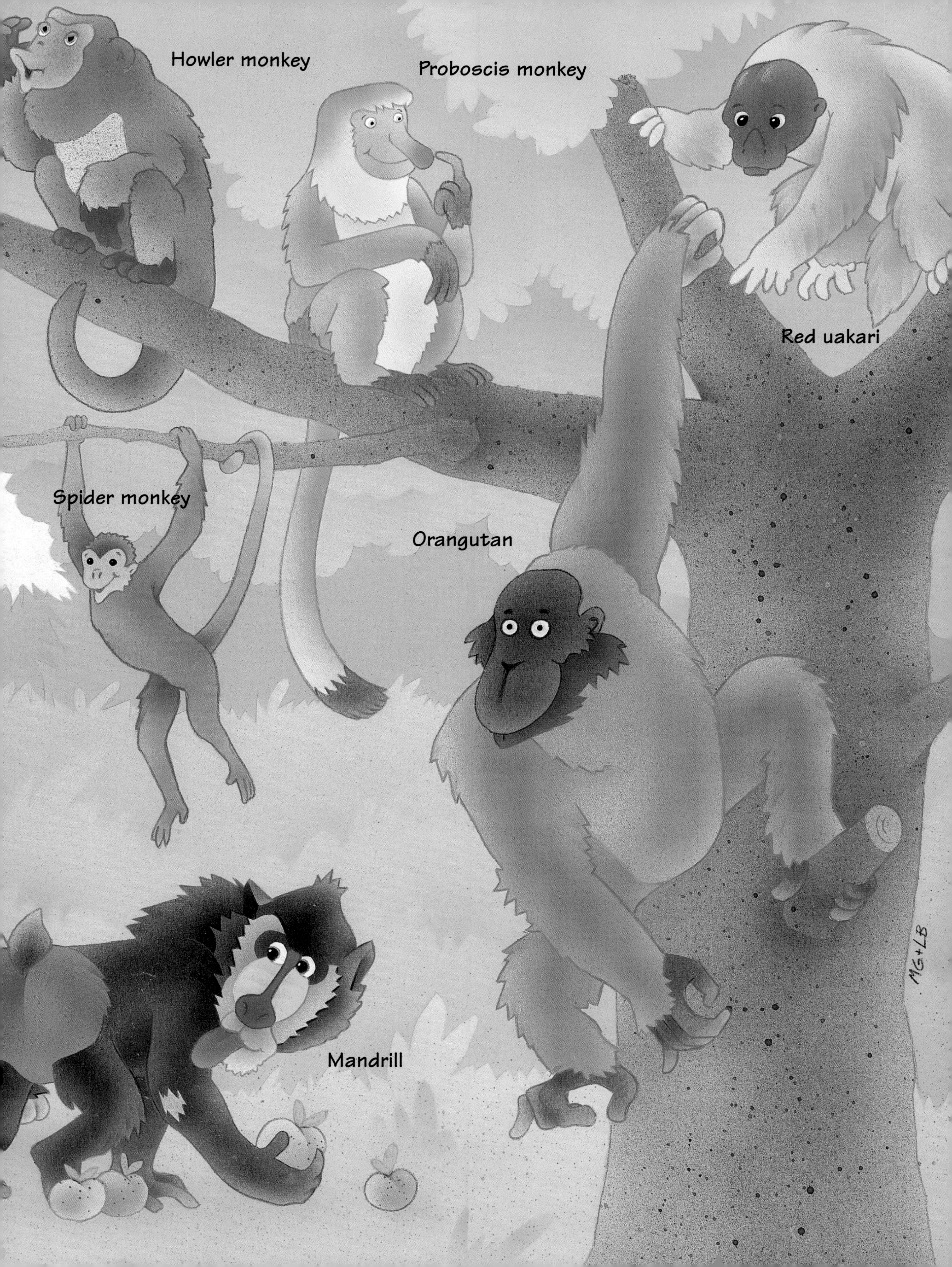
Howler monkey
Proboscis monkey
Red uakari
Spider monkey
Orangutan
Mandrill
MG+LB

THE MOST LIKABLE

The CHIMPANZEE is the nearest in intelligence to humans, so it's not surprising that this is one of the most studied and popular apes. Unlike most animals, chimpanzees use tools: they use sticks to help them dig honey from trees or ants from their nests, and they use stones to crack nuts and throw at intruders. They eat mostly fruit, leaves, and roots, although scientists have found that some chimpanzees also like meat.

THE MOST COLORFUL

The male MANDRILL looks just like a circus clown, funny and colorful. But he has a short temper and the least annoyance will soon have him baring a mouthful of sharp teeth, almost as deadly as those of his greatest enemy, the lion.

THE MOST HUMAN

ORANGUTAN means, in the language of Borneo, 'man of the forest'. Years ago, people thought that's what he was, from skeletons they had found. Today we know that orangutans are apes, taller and heavier than men. They are very intelligent and peaceful creatures. They are able to walk on two legs, but prefer to travel on all fours, or swing from tree to tree. The male orangutan even grows a moustache and beard, although the rest of his face is hairless.

THE MOST RIDICULOUS

The PROBOSCIS MONKEY gets its name from its enormous nose. Male monkeys have noses up to 8 inches long, and they use these noses to make very loud noises! They make these noises to scare off intruders and to attract mates. Females prefer husbands with the biggest noses and noisiest calls. Proboscis monkeys live in Borneo, often near rivers where they love to dive and swim.

THE MOST EASILY SEEN

The RED UAKARI doesn't have much hair on its face. It's about as large as a cat, has a short tail, and lives in the trees of the Amazonian forest, where it tries in vain to hide itself in the green leaves. This is difficult because of its brilliant orange hair and the color of the skin on its face which varies from pink to scarlet. Local Indians often like to capture these animals to keep as pets.

THE BEST EQUIPPED

The monkey is said to have four hands because it can use its back and front legs as true hands. You could say that the SPIDER MONKEY has five hands: its very long tail helps it to move in the Venezuelan forest with great skill. Hanging by its tail, it can easily use its other four hands to reach the leaves and fruit it likes to eat. The spider monkey is quite an acrobat in the trees but, because its tail is so much longer than its body, it finds it difficult to walk comfortably on the ground.

THE SMALLEST

The PYGMY MARMOSET, at less than 6 inches long, is the smallest monkey in the world. It lives only in the Amazon region, moving like a squirrel in the trees and feeding on insects, fruit and leaves. With its likable face and tiny size it looks quite lovable, but this little creature has a bad temper and can be extremely fierce.

THE BEST WALKER

The GIBBON walks on two legs nearly as well as a man, without the need of support from the hands as other apes do. It prefers to live in trees, however, where it loves to show off. You will often find groups of gibbons doing acrobatics worthy of a circus, throwing themselves into the air from one branch to another, without a net. Although small, the gibbon is not easily defeated. Even tigers will avoid an argument with these animals.

THE NOISIEST

The HOWLER MONKEY lets out the most amazing scream you are ever likely to hear in the South American forests. These monkeys live in groups and usually start the day with a good yell! But these piercing shouts are used for many reasons. The oldest monkey acts as lookout for the others, and howls if danger is near. If an intruder does approach, a few more screeches soon scare it off. And, of course, if one monkey wants to talk to another one across the group—it yells!

THE BIGGEST

The male GORILLA can be up to 6 feet tall and weigh up to 440 pounds. He could be the gold-medal weight lifter of the apes and, if enemies approach, he often beats his broad chest with his hands, making a drumming sound that soon scares them off. Gorillas may seem aggressive, but they are really intelligent, family-loving animals, rarely needing to prove their strength. They live on fruit and other plants and don't often need to drink water as they get most of what they need from their food.

Tree frog ♂
Dance fly ♂
♀ Frigatebirds
Moose ♂
♂ Grea
grebe
Fiddler crabs
♀
♂
♂
Stickleb.

THE GREAT ROMANTICS

Just like humans, some animals will do almost anything to attract a mate. The way they look, the things they do and the noises they make can be quite amazing!

THE MOST GRACEFUL

The GREAT CRESTED GREBE is a bird that lives in ponds and marshlands, feeding on fish, frogs, and insects. When he decides to start a family he changes the color of his neck plumage from grey to red, and he displays tufts of black feathers at the sides of his head. Then he invites his chosen mate to dance. Together they twirl around on the surface of the water, bending their necks into S-shapes and using their webbed feet as paddles. They also offer each other food, usually bunches of tasty weeds.

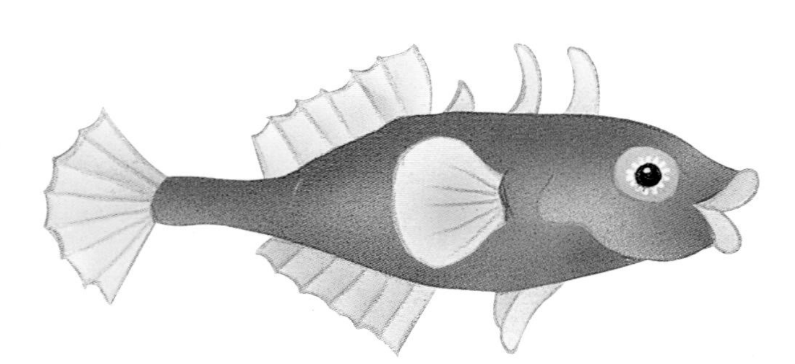

THE LIVELIEST

The STICKLEBACK is a small, spiny fish that lives both in fresh and sea water. When this male decides to attract a mate, he too does a dance, twisting and wriggling in the water. In case the female misses this, he also turns a lively red colour. While he is dancing, the stickleback carefully chooses a spot for a nest. He then produces a thread from his body and weaves all the plants in that area into a kind of nest. This is where the females he attracts will lay their eggs.

THE MOST UNSELFISH

The MALE DANCE FLY is a generous gentleman. He attracts female dance flies with charming gifts of little insects, wrapped up in a silken cocoon he has made himself. This gift is difficult to make because the whole operation has to be performed in the air; his legs are too thin and weak to walk. In fact, he doesn't fly too well either, because his wings are quite delicate. Sometimes the female will discover that the wrapping is empty because the male has failed to catch any insects, but as they say it's the thought that counts!

THE MOST STRIKING

The FRIGATEBIRD is a large sea bird whose feathers are practically all smoky black, so when he wants to attract a mate he has to do something that makes him stand out in a crowd. His trick is to puff out the red feathers on his throat so they flash brighter than a traffic light at nights! As if that wasn't enough, he also gives out ear-piercing cries and shakes his wings, which are more than 6 feet long. When the female can't resist him any longer, she lovingly rubs her beak on his feathers and rests her head on his bright red throat.

THE NOISIEST

The TREE FROG is an expert climber with a slender body, long legs, and round toes with suckers that help them cling to branches. The male is not very big, until he starts to look for a mate. Then he puffs up his throat, like a balloon, until it is larger in size than his head. At the same time he makes a series of bell-like gurgles that any passing female cannot possibly ignore. Once the tree frog has attracted his mate, they both dive into the water where the female will lay hundreds of eggs. When this has happened, the frogs return to their homes in the trees, silent once more.

THE MOST MUSICAL

CRICKETS are so small that, even if they grew red throats and antlers, then danced madly, the females still wouldn't notice them because they are dark night-time animals and live hidden in tall grass. So the little males 'sing' love songs to their sweethearts, by rubbing their legs and wing cases together. The music varies in rhythm and loudness, depending on the temperature and how far away the loved ones are.

THE QUIETEST

The FIDDLER CRAB lives on the coasts of the Indian and Pacific Oceans, well protected in holes in the sand which are sealed with stones and empty shells. Every so often the male comes out to eat (he likes algae and little fish) and to look for a wife. One of his front claws is much bigger than the other and he often looks as though he is carrying a violin under his chin, which is why he got his name. When he meets a female, he uses this claw to wave to her several times, beckoning her into his home.

THE CLUMSIEST

The male MOOSE is very proud of his enormous antlers and every year he gets rid of the old ones and replaces them with brand new ones, always a little larger than the last set. Sometimes the old horns do not fall off at the right time and so the beast angrily bashes them against tree trunks, trying to break them. This is a difficult operation as they are very large, usually more than 3 feet high and up to 44 pounds in weight. The new horns are an irresistible attraction for the females, who do not have antlers. In addition to the antlers, the male moose begins a frenzied dance and produces a terrible mooing sound. If two males are interested in the same female, this can often end in a noisy and frantic battle, until one at last runs away.

GREAT GREAT GRANDFATHERS

Over many millions of years, the animals on earth have adapted and changed to the forms we know today. The same is true for human beings. Long after the dinosaurs died out, but longer ago than anyone alive today can remember, the first people lived on earth. Let's take a look at what some of them were like.

Homo sapiens sapiens
Homo sapiens sapiens
neanderthalensis
Homo habilis
Australopithecus
africanus
Australopithecus
afarensis
MG+GC

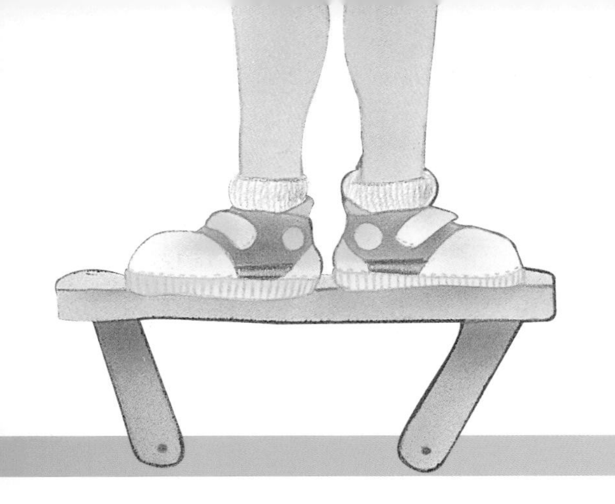

THE MOST INTELLIGENT

The most intelligent of all the animals that appeared on earth about 35,000 years ago, HOMO SAPIENS SAPIENS was the most intelligent. This group spread rapidly throughout the world, destroying enemies whether they were man or beast. This man developed weapons and used nature by breeding animals and growing food. He learned to dress himself, build fortified houses, and improve his lifestyle. We are his direct grandchildren and we continue to combat every enemy (natural or not) to survive.

THE OLDEST ANCESTOR

The oldest ancestor of man was ANCESTRAL APE. Small and agile, he lived about 5 million years ago. When his forest home was destroyed he was forced to live in the savannah (open ground with few trees) and learned to move rapidly on his back legs. Although no remains have been found of this race, scientists have no doubt that he actually existed.

THE FIRST TRUE HOMINID

The first true hominid, that is the first animal that we think possessed characteristics and attitudes like ours, was the AUSTRALOPITHECUS AFARENSIS. About the size of a 6-year-old child, he had a bulging jaw, a low forehead and arched eyebrows: a look very similar to that of the chimpanzee. He knew how to walk on his back legs (but helping himself with his hands) and he possessed a brain a little larger than that of a modern monkey. He lived, eating roots and sticks, on the plains of East Africa about 3.5 million years ago.

THE FIRST CRAFTSMAN

The first craftsman was probably the AUSTRALOPITHECUS AFRICANUS. Numbers of scientists consider him the grandchild of the *Australopithecus afarensis* as he was of more or less the same size and look, with long, sharp front teeth, smaller than a monkey's. He may have lived in communities, hunting in groups. He would also have lived on fruit, seeds, and roots. Proof of his advanced intelligence is found in traces of chipped bone, formed into rough but useful tools. He also lived in East Africa, about 2.5 million years ago.

THE UNLUCKIEST

The unluckiest of the hominids AUSTRALOPITHECUS ROBUSTUS, so called because of his muscles, weighed approximately 110 pounds. He looked particularly ape-like, especially with his bony forehead. He was a peaceful vegetarian, hunted by tigers and bears, so this race died out about 1 million years ago. In reality he is not one of our direct ancestors, only a distant cousin. He lived mostly in Southern or Central East Africa.

THE FIRST SCULPTOR

HOMO HABILIS was the first man ever to make things out of stone. He made weapons, tools, and bowls which would seem nothing to us, but were great prizes to him. He had a small build but a head and brain bigger than any man before him. Some scientists believe that he was able to make sounds—'speaking' in his own way. He lived in East Africa (and perhaps in Southeast Asia) about 1.5 million years ago.

THE FIRST INHABITANT

The first inhabitant of the earth with a similar look to ours was the HOMO ERECTUS. He was small (5 feet tall), but he was however very 'human', with a brain almost as large as ours. He roamed as a hunter and gatherer of leaves and berries, and he could build shelters with wooden walls, supported by beams and blocks of stone. He also made weapons from wood, horn, bones, and stones. But most important of all, he learned to light a fire and used it for cooking meat and to defend himself from enemies.
He lived in Africa, Europe and Asia 1.5 million years ago.

THE MOST REFINED

HOMO SAPIENS NEANDERTHALENSIS was a very intelligent early man. He was an able artist and sculptor of stones and ivory. When someone of this group died, he was buried in a tomb. They probably had some form of religion because they believed that the cave bear was a god. He had a peaceful nature and was killed out almost certainly by the more brutal and warlike *Homo sapiens*. He lived between 250,000 and 30,000 years ago in Europe, Asia and North Africa.

THE ANIMALS MOST LIKE MAN

The animals most like man are the anthropoid (or man-like) apes, and from these the ORANGUTAN, CHIMPANZEE, and GORILLA are the most 'human'. They are able to use primitive tools. They can communicate between themselves, and they live in social and organized communities.

ANIMAL INDEX